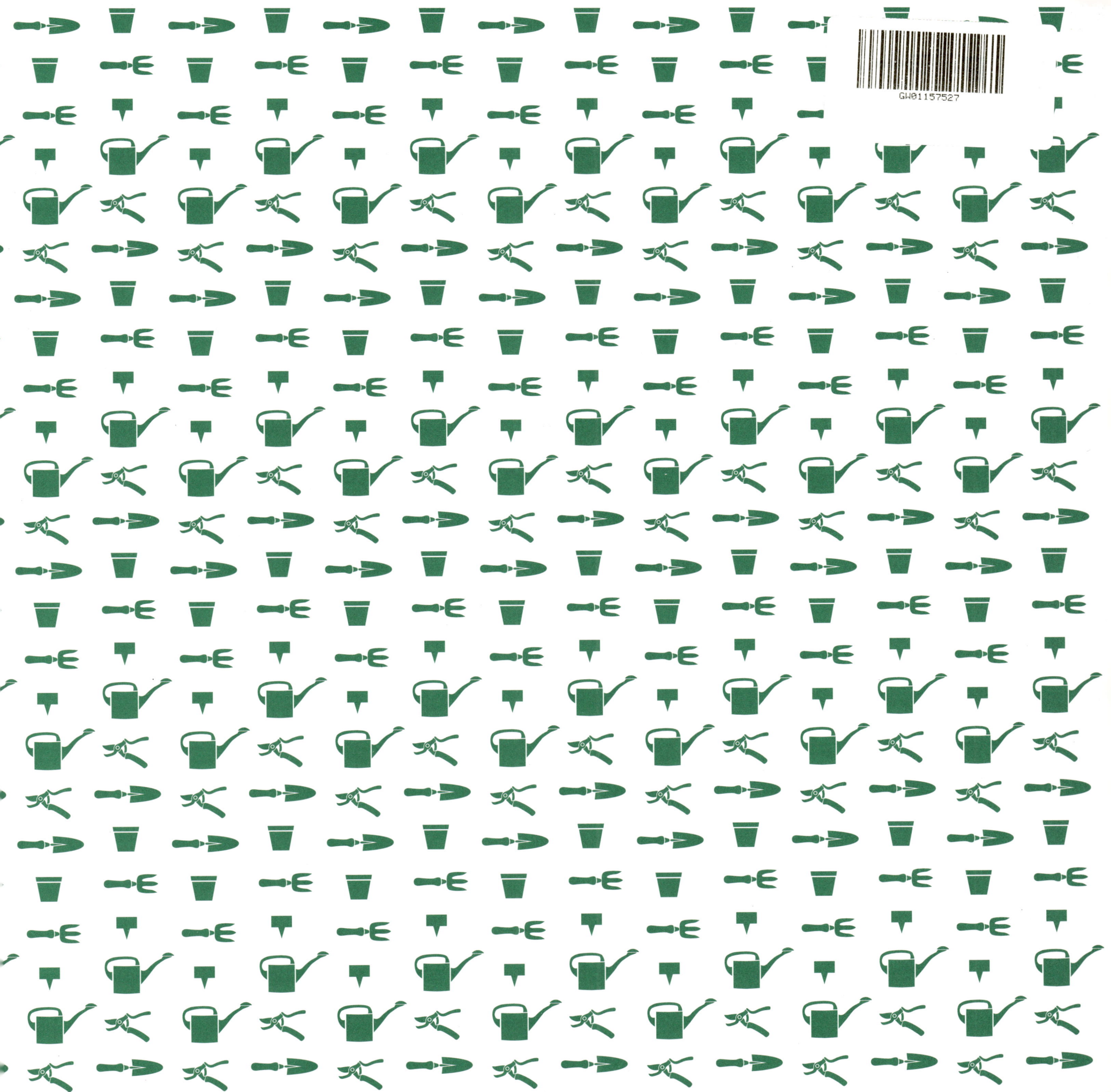

Start to plant
HERB GARDENS

Create your ideal garden with these simple-to-follow projects

Graham A. Pavey

APPLE

A QUINTET BOOK

Published by The Apple Press
6 Blundell Street
London N7 9BH

Copyright © 1996 Quintet Publishing Limited.
All rights reserved. No part of this publication may
be reproduced, stored in a retrieval system or
transmitted in any form or by any means,
electronic, mechanical, photocopying, recording
or otherwise, without the permission of the
copyright holder.

ISBN 1-85076-648-7

This book was designed and produced by
Quintet Publishing Limited
6 Blundell Street
London N7 9BH

Creative Director: Richard Dewing
Designer: James Lawrence
Project Editor: Diana Steedman
Editor: Janet Swarbrick
Photographer: Keith Waterton

Typeset in Great Britain by
Central Southern Typesetters, Eastbourne
Manufactured by Bright Arts (Singapore) Pte Ltd
Printed by Leefung-Asco Printers Ltd, China

Author's Acknowledgements

I would like to give special thanks to Dave, Jason and Paul of DJ Landscapes, 28 Wingfield Road, Bromham, Beds.; to Sandra and Richard Oliver, Angela Whiting, Barry Johnson and all the staff at Anglia Alpines and Herbs Ltd, St Ives Road, Somersham, Huntingdon, Cambs. PE17 3ET; Maureen Cattlin and the staff at Milton Ernest Garden Centre, Radwell Road, Milton Ernest, Beds. MK44 1SH; and to Steve Woods and the staff at Tacchi's Garden Scene, Wyton, Huntingdon, Cambs. PE17 2AA.

Picture Credits

The Publisher would like to thank the following for providing photographs and for permission to reproduce copyright material.
Graham A. Pavey: *pp. 5, 6, 7, 8, 14, 38, 39, 42, 43, 44, 45.*
Garden Matters: *pp. 4, 6, 9, 11, 15, 26, 34, 38, 42, 43, 46.*
Harry Smith Collection: *pp. 7, 26, 38, 43, 45.*

Contents

Introduction...*4*

Materials and Techniques...*5*

Herb Cascade...*11*

Herb Ladder...*14*

Herb Pots...*19*

Mint Diamonds...*22*

Herb Wheel...*26*

Herbs In Paving...*30*

Hanging Basket...*34*

Herb Border...*38*

Herbs In A Mixed Border...*42*

Window Box...*46*

INTRODUCTION

Parsley, sage, rosemary and thyme are just some of the aromatic herbs, with their culinary, perfumery or medicinal uses that have been cultivated through the centuries, from the earliest monastic and physic gardens to their more recent revival as easy-to-grow, ornamental plants. With careful selection, and a little imagination, herbs can be used to enhance our gardens and homes as well as serving a practical purpose.

In this book we explore ways of using herbs to their fullest potential. Plants like mugwort, horseradish or horehound, which serve little useful purpose and can become serious pests in the garden, are not used. The herbs in this book are useful in the kitchen or for their scent and as decorative and ornamental plants for the flower garden.

From the traditional herb wheel through to the more innovative herb cascade, the projects offer something for every gardener. There are larger projects, which can be incorporated into the overall design of a garden, and simple schemes designed to provide a quick and easy method of making herbs available to the kitchen.

MATERIALS & TECHNIQUES

The Herbs

Many herbs are invasive colonizers, either by underground root systems or by seed. Several of the designs in this book show herbs grown in segments separated by brick or paving, a method which helps to contain the plants' roots. In some instances, especially with the mints, it may be necessary to plant the herb inside a bucket or container. This must be at least 12 in/30 cm deep with the bottom removed. Plants which spread rapidly by seed, like golden feverfew, are best clipped when the flowers appear to stop them setting seed.

For most projects, the smallest plants will be suitable, but some plants, like rosemary and sage, unless for a special use, are better purchased as much larger specimens. Plants are usually sold by the size of the pot they are grown in 3½ in/9 cm being the smallest. The recommended plant size is shown against the plant in each project.

Most of the herbs in this book can be used in the kitchen, bathroom or medicine chest, while others are purely ornamental.

Angelica Candied angelica is used as a cake decoration. Angelica leaves are also good for adding to rhubarb instead of sugar.
Artemisia "Powis Castle" The beautiful silvery grey foliage of this plant is a perfect foil for green-leaved herbs. Its close relative, wormwood, can be used as a moth repellent.

Angelica (*Angelica archangelica*).

Basil This plant comes in many different varieties, with a wide range of leaf colour and shape. It is a good accompaniment to meat, eggs, mushrooms and tomatoes, and an integral part of Italian cooking, adding flavour to pasta and pizzas.

Bay (*Laurus nobilis*).

Bay Used in soups, stews and stocks containing fish, meat, poultry and game. The fresh leaves have a stronger flavour than the dried ones.

Bergamot (*Monarda didyma*).

Bergamot This showy herb is just as easily at home in a mixed flower border as in a herb garden. The leaves can be added sparingly to salads and are a good accompaniment to pork.

Bergamot flowers keep their fragrance and colour when dried and are an important ingredient for pot-pourris.

The first herbal was published in America in 1569 by Nicholas Monardes. Bergamot (Monarda didyma) commemorates him. The native Americans, who introduced the settlers to many new herbs, used it to make a tea called Oswego.

Camomile (*Chamaemelum nobile*).

Camomile Mainly used for cosmetics and medicines, it can also be used to make camomile tea, which is said to improve the appetite. Camomile oil added to bath water will aid relaxation.

Caraway The seeds are used in pies, biscuits, bread and apple dishes, whilst the root can be cooked as a vegetable.

Catmint (*Nepeta racemosa*).

Catmint Catmint has some medicinal properties. It is much loved by cats who enjoy rolling in it.

Chervil One of the "fines herbes", much used in French cuisine, it has a delicate flavour with a touch of aniseed. Use leaves in salads, soups, sauces, vegetables, chicken and fish dishes.

Chives (*Allium schoenoprasum*).

Chives Good in soups, fish, egg dishes, cream cheese and with potatoes. It is also used in salads where the edible purple flowers can be used for decoration.

Coriander Two parts of this plant are of use. The leaves can be used sparingly to garnish salads, curries, stews and sauces, and the seeds, which have a different flavour, are used to flavour curries, rice, tomato and avocado dishes.

Curry plant (*Helichrysum italicum*).

Curry Plant Although the leaves have a strong scent, it is lost in cooking, but they can be added to rice and vegetables after cooking to introduce a mild curry flavour.

Fennel (*Foeniculum vulgare*).

Fennel Fennel is good with fish, pork, veal, chicken and young vegetables. In the garden fennel attracts hoverflies, voracious feeders of whitefly, so making a practical, as well as a culinary and ornamental contribution.

Tarragon (*Artemisia dracunculus*).

French tarragon This is a good accompaniment to many foods, including veal, poultry and game, shellfish, egg dishes, vegetables and tomatoes. Henry VIII is believed to have divorced Catherine of Aragon for her reckless use of the herb!

French tarragon is best planted in a bottomless flower pot or bucket to help contain its invasive underground runners.

Golden feverfew (*Tanacetum parthenium*).

Golden feverfew Used in medicine, mainly for treating migraines, this plant has no culinary use.

Roast-beef plant (*Iris foetidissima*).

Roast beef plant (*Iris foetidissima*) Grown as an ornamental plant, the spiky leaves and bright orange berries in the autumn add height and colour to a border even in quite deep shade.

Lady's mantle (*Alchemilla mollis*).

Lady's mantle Used by herbalists to treat menstrual disorders, there are no culinary uses for this plant, but it is an attractive addition to the flower garden.

Golden marjoram (*Origanum vulgare* "Aureum").

Marjoram Marjoram, or oregano, combines well with tomato, meat and pizza dishes and is the main ingredient of bouquet garni.

Moroccan mint (*Mentha spicata*).

Applemint (*Mentha suaveolens*).

Spearmint (*Mentha spicata*).

Mint There are many species of mint available to the gardener. It is good with mutton, lamb, veal, fish, potatoes and peas, and in drinks and fruit cups. Mint has long been cultivated for its aromatic, culinary and antiseptic qualities. Nearly all are invasive creeping plants, and are best planted in bottomless containers to curb their spreading underground roots.

Parsley (*Petrosalinium sativus*).

Parsley Excellent for use in soups and stews and with lamb, parsley is also good with fish and in stuffing for poultry and game. Omelettes and vegetables benefit from the addition of some parsley and it is used as a garnish to many dishes.

Rosemary (*Rosmarinus officinalis*).

Rosemary Ideal for use with pork, lamb and chicken, rosemary is also cultivated for its aromatic oils. Rosemary can be grown as a hedge, the clippings dried and used in the kitchen throughout the year.

Rue This bitter herb is cultivated for its decorative, glaucous leaves and is held to have magical properties – particularly if obtained by theft.

LEFT: Golden Sage (*Salvia officinalis* "Icterina").
RIGHT: Sage (*Salvia officinalis*).

Sage An excellent accompaniment for pork, goose, duck and oily fish, sage has deliciously aromatic foliage and is widely cultivated for medicinal uses.

Sweet Cicely The root can be cooked as a vegetable or eaten raw. The leaves have an aniseed flavour and can be added to salads or chopped and added to soups and stews.

Soapwort or tumbing Ted This plant has no culinary uses, but is used medicinally to treat skin conditions.

Strawberry Strawberries are very ornamental plants and any variety can be used to brighten up a herb garden. The fruit can be used in salads, desserts or simply eaten on their own. A tea can be made from the leaves.

Thyme (*Thymus* "Doone Valley").

Thyme Thymes are good in soups, meat stews, stuffing for poultry, salads and also combines well with fish and vegetables. They retain their fragrance well on drying and are used in pot-pourris and herb pillows. In the Middle Ages thyme was a symbol of courage, and high-ranking ladies embroidered sprigs on to the clothes of knights off to the Crusades.

Building Materials

Bricks come in a range of hardness, from very soft stock bricks to very hard engineering bricks. The softer the bricks, the more prone they are to attack by frost. Softer bricks have a more pleasing texture and may be desirable from a design point of view. Frost damaged bricks can also be a feature in themselves. If using soft bricks, buy some extra ones for use at a later date to replace any breakages. House bricks would a good choice, but there is a wide range of materials, from concrete pavers to granite setts. The key is to ensure that they fit with your overall plan.

Use spirit level and lump hammer to ensure bricks are laid flat.

Hardcore consists of any form of rubble, broken up with the lump hammer and squashed into place at the base of an excavation, ready for laying paving. Old bricks, concrete, stones or any solid waste material could be used.

Lean mix is 6 parts builder's sand to 1 part cement with a little water added to damp it down slightly and make it easy to use. This mixture will dry to a solid base. When pointing between the bricks care should be taken to avoid soiling the brick face.

Concrete cement mix is 6 parts builder's sand to 1 part cement mixed with water to form a cake-mix consistency. It is used for laying paving slabs.

Soils

Herbs are diverse in their soil requirements. Many are sun-lovers enjoying dry impoverished conditions, but some, such as parsley, require better treatment.

The best approach is not to feed the soil, but to deal with the hungry plants individually. If you have a clay soil, it would be beneficial to break this up by digging in sharp sand to improve drainage, but do not go any deeper than a spade's depth as you may bring some undesirable subsoil to the surface.

For containers **peat-based compost** has the advantage of being light, so is ideal in hanging baskets and containers which are intended to be moved around. The disadvantage is that it dries out very quickly. Because the extraction of peat and the damage to peat bogs is environmentally unsound, seek out a manufacturer with a sound policy of obtaining peat from managed peat bogs.

Peat-based compost.   *Soil-based compost.*

Moss.   CENTRE: *Shredded forest bark.*   *Sharp sand.*

Alternative composts, based on shredded forest bark, are viable alternatives, as is coir, or coconut fibre, although the extraction of this too, is said to be having a detrimental effect on its native soil.

Soil-based compost is heavier and is best used in containers which are permanently sited. It has the advantage of remaining moist longer.

Moss is used to line hanging baskets. It is easily obtainable from garden centres or an alternative source is moss raked from the lawn, but you must ensure that no chemicals have been used to treat the grass.

Sharp sand should be dug into heavy, clay soils to break up the texture and improve drainage. Any clean sand could be used instead, but avoid yellow builder's sand as this can be very dirty and greasy.

Plant Care

Regular maintenance of plants will help keep their attractive appearance.

Watering herbs regularly is important but many herbs from hot dry countries have aromatic oils in their leaves and stems, which help to reduce water loss through evaporation, and enable the plant to cope with dry conditions more effectively. Many herbs need less watering than other plants and will tolerate neglect. There are some exceptions and these are indicated in each project. The ability to cope with dry conditions makes many herbs perfect subjects for containers.

Watering should, ideally, be carried out first thing in the morning. Care should be taken to avoid splashing water on the leaves as this can cause them to scorch in the sun.

Regular maintenance of plants will help to keep their attractive appearance. Many herbs start off the growing season looking fresh and inviting, but by late summer become scruffy. This usually happens when they have set seed, so the first solution is to trim off any flower stems that appear, or deadhead regularly. This will help to keep the plant bushy and encourage new growth.

The drastic and final solution is to cut the plant down to the ground, which removes it until the next season, or, if it is grown in a container, remove it to a place out of sight.

Tools and equipment

Use a **garden trowel** for digging holes for planting small plants.

A **garden rake** should be used to prepare the soil surface once an area of soil has been dug over. The surface is raked, to create a fine tilth ready for planting, by dragging the rake backwards and forwards across the area.

You will need a **spade** for digging over beds and borders before planting, and for planting larger plant specimens.

A **wheelbarrow** is essential for moving soil and sand around when preparing a border. It is also useful for mixing sand and cement ready for use.

Crocks are needed for drainage in the bottom of containers. The best are broken bits of terracotta flowerpots, although broken tiles or medium-sized stones collected from the garden would also suffice.

A **builder's line** is a very useful piece of equipment to ensure the bricks are laid in a straight line. One can be made with strong cord and two wooden stakes.

Use a **spirit level** to ensure that any bricks or paving are laid flat.

A **stake** such as a short piece of wood, or metal, or a tent peg with line attached is used as the centre point for marking out a circle.

A **lump hammer** is needed throughout the projects for levelling bricks and paving.

A **builder's trowel** is used for mixing and placing cement and is essential for pointing between bricks or paving.

Herb Cascade

This unusual way of growing herbs was discovered in an old Victorian gardening book. As well as herbs, alpines and bedding plants can be grown in this way and the effect can be quite stunning.

The ideal place for the herb cascade would be close to the kitchen door or even in a conservatory, where the herbs could easily be harvested as required. It could also be used as part of a group of containers on a patio.

Materials

Five terracotta flower pots, one each of diameter 15½ in/39 cm; 13 in/32 cm; 10½ in/27 cm; 8 in/21 cm; and 6½ in/16 cm • Crocks • Peat-based compost

CARE

Although most of the plants in this scheme are perennials, they may need replacing each spring to keep the arrangement fresh. The parsley will need replacing each year.

The Plants

A. *3 alpine strawberry (Fragaria vesca "Semperflorens"), 3½ in/9 cm pots*

B. *3 thyme (Thymus serpyllum coccineus "Major"), 3½ in/9 cm pots*

C. *3 parsley (Petroselinum crispum), 3½ in/9 cm pots*

D. *2 chives (Allium schoenoprasum) 3½ in/9 cm pots*

E. *1 silver mint (Mentha longifolia), 3½ in/9 cm pots*

Start to plant • HERB GARDENS

1. Starting with the largest pot, cover base of pot with a generous layer of crocks to aid drainage.

2. Add peat-based or lightweight compost so the arrangement will not be too heavy to move.

3. Bring compost up to a level where the second pot will sit comfortably with the base of its rim against the top of the first pot. Keep trying the pot out until the desired level is found.

4. Ensuring the second pot is firmly held in place against the back of the first pot, fill in with compost, firming and consolidating to ensure a solid fit. The occasional tap against the pot will help to settle the compost.

5. Repeat the process with the other pots until the whole cascade is completed.

Planting Plan

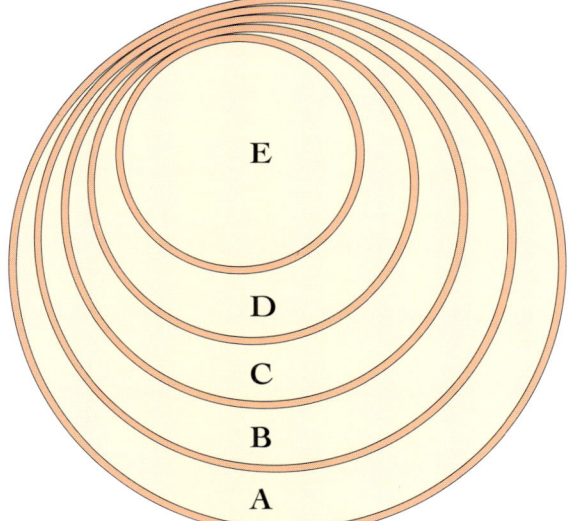

1. Starting on the bottom tier, carefully plant up each level. Tease out the roots of each plant before you plant it to ensure that they quickly start to grow into the new compost. Plant the 3 alpine strawberry plants in Pot A.
2. Next plant the 3 thymes in Pot B.
3. The 3 parsley plants should be planted in Pot C.
4. In Pot D, plant the 2 chives.
5. The cascade is topped with a silver mint planted in Pot E. The completed cascade will quickly mature if planted in the spring.

ALTERNATIVE PLANTING SCHEME

Pot A.
3 golden marjoram (*Origanum vulgare* "Aureum"), 3½in/9cm pots

Pot B.
3 soapwort or tumbling Ted (*Saponaria ocymoides*), 3½in/9cm pots

Pot C.
2 chives (*Allium schoenoprasum*), 3½in/9cm pots

Pot D.
3 purple basil (*Ocimum basilicum* var. *purpurascens*), 3½in/9cm pots

Pot E.
1 rosemary (*Rosmarinus officinalis*), 5½in/1 litre pot

Herb Ladder

This traditional design is a very flexible way of growing herbs in a large area. The space between each "rung" provides a segment where the more invasive plants can be restrained and the bricks make it easy to access each plant. The scheme can be made larger by adding more "rungs" or adding a second ladder alongside the first. The perfect setting for a herb ladder in the garden, would be alongside a path or patio, perhaps forming an interlock between the hard surface and a flower border. As the plants mature, the sages and camomile will grow over the brickwork and path, blurring and softening the hard edges.

By using the same brick in the ladder, as that used in the construction of the house you can create a "link" between the house and the garden.

The Plants

A. *6 camomile (Chamaemelum nobile "Treneague"), 3½ in/9 cm pots*

D. *2 purple sage (Salvia officinalis "Purpurescens"), 6½ in/2 litre or 8½ in/3 litre pots*

G. *3 golden feverfew (Tanacetum parthenium "Aureum"), 3½ in/9 cm pots*

B. *2 golden sage (Salvia officinalis "Icterina"), 6½ in/2 litre or 8½ in/3 litre pots*

E. *2 chives (Allium schoenoprasum), 3½ in/9 cm or 5½ in/1 litre pots*

H. *1 curry plant (Helichrysum italicum), 3½ in/9 cm or 5½ in/1 litre pot*

C. *1 rue (Ruta Graveolens "Jackman's Blue"), 5½ in/1 litre or 6½ in/2 litre pot*

F. *1 French tarragon (Artemisia dracunculus), 5½ in/1 litre or 6½ in/2 litre pot*

I. *1 bronze fennel (Foeniculum vulgare "Purpureum"), 3½ in/9cm or 5½ in/1 litre pot*

Materials

90 bricks • Lean mix (1 part cement to 6 parts builder's sand) • Builders line • Spirit level • Lump hammer • Spade • Builder's trowel • Garden trowel

J. 2 lemon thyme (*Thymus × citriodorus* "Aureus"), 3½ in/9cm pots

K. 1 apple mint (*Mentha suaveolens*), 6½ in/2 litre or 8½ in/3 litre pot

L. 1 basil (*Ocimum basilicum*), 3½ in/9cm or 5½ in/1 litre pot

M. 2 parsley (*Petroselinum crispum*), 3½ in/9 cm pots

1. Start with the "uprights" of the ladder. Dig out a trench 9ft/3m in length by 2ft/0.5m wide.

3. A spirit level will keep the bricks on an even keel. Use 31 bricks.

2. Begin to lay the bricks onto a dry mix base. Use a builders line to ensure a straight run.

4. Having completed the first "upright" of the ladder, the second can be laid parallel to the first and 4 bricks apart. Keep checking the distance between the "uprights" as the bricks are laid to ensure they are parallel.

5. Install the "rungs" of the ladder.

6. Lay the plants out ready for planting by following the Planting Plan.

1. Tease out the roots of each plant before you plant it.

In Segment 1 plant the 6 camomile plants (A). This variety of camomile forms a low ground-hugging mat and is commonly used to create camomile lawns. Here, it has been selected to offer a low contrast to the sage and rue in the second segment and to soften the brickwork at one end.

2. In Segment 2 plant 1 golden sage (B). This sage has green and golden variegated leaves. It will grow out over the brickwork forming a low mound. The colour and texture of the leaves will provide a good companion for the rue and the chives (in Segment 3).

Next, plant the rue (C). This herb, used only for medicinal purposes, has great ornamental use. It combines well with roses and herbaceous plants. Here its powder blue, finely divided leaves provide a contrast in shape and texture to those of the accompanying sages. *Warning: handling this plant can cause an allergic reaction. Care should be taken not to touch the leaves when planting or collecting sage for the kitchen.*

In front of the rue, still in Segment 2, plant 1 purple sage (D). This sage has purple leaves and the same form as the golden sage.

3. In Segment 3 plant 1 chives (E). As well as being one of the best culinary herbs, the attractive chive flowers contribute much to any planting scheme. The grass-like leaves

Planting Plan

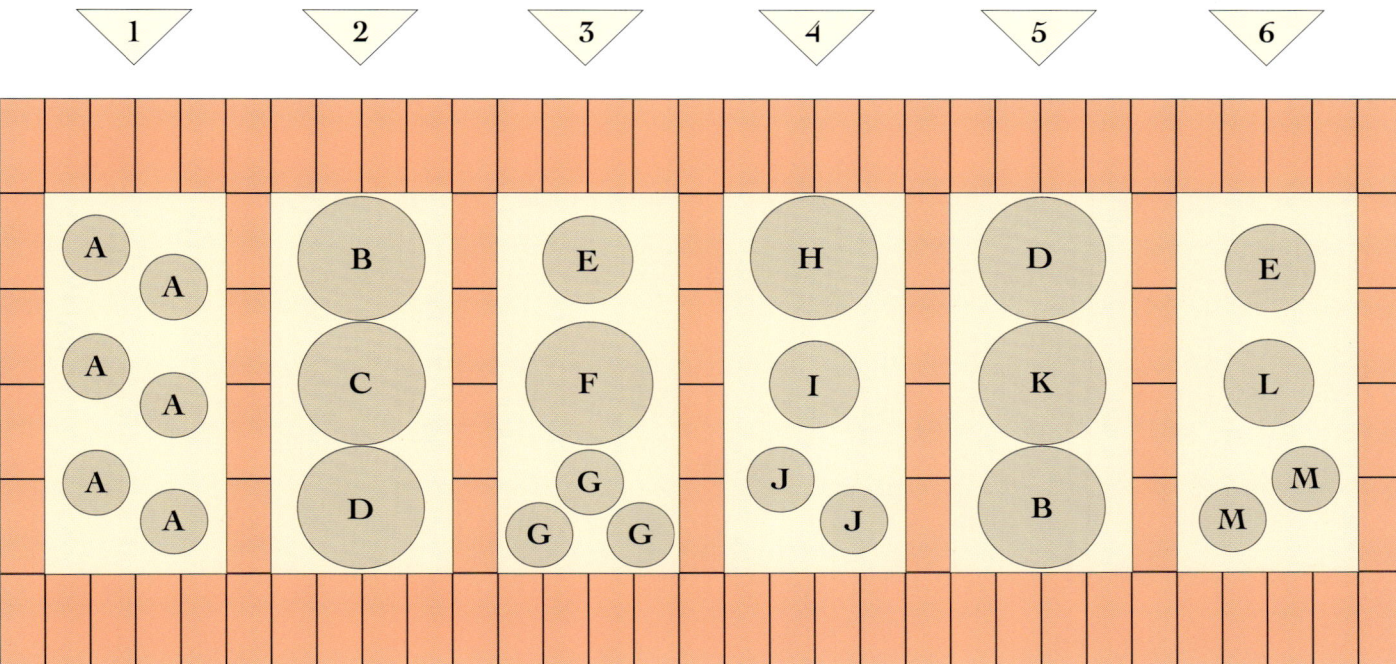

contrast well with the grey-leaved curry plant and the upright French tarragon.

Next plant the French tarragon (F). By planting it in the centre, the surrounding plants will help to mask it later in the season when it can become very untidy. The plant produces invasive underground runners and is therefore best planted in a large flower pot or old bucket, with the bottom removed.

Plant the 3 golden feverfew (G) in a group. In the spring nothing can compete with golden feverfew for its bright freshness. It loses some colour as the season goes by, but trimming it over occasionally encourages fresh growth. Here it will contrast well with the purple sage in Segment 2 and pick up the colours of the lemon thyme in Segment 4.

4. In Segment 4 plant the curry plant (H). Unlike many grey leaved plants, the curry plant looks good all the year round. Here it will contrast with the feathery leaves of the bronze fennel and the textured leaves of the sage. Trimming the plant occasionally will encourage it to bush out.

Next plant the bronze fennel (I). This perennial is commonly used in mixed flower borders where its tall feathery form offers a contrast to many border plants. Fennel attracts hoverflies, a voracious predator of whitefly which has a taste for basil, and thereby makes a practical contribution to the garden as well as a culinary and ornamental one.

Plant the 2 lemon thyme (J). This variety has a strong lemon scent and the bonus of pink flowers in midsummer. Here, the golden yellow leaves pick up the golden theme from the sage in Segment 2 and Segment 5 and the golden feverfew in Segment 3.

There is a vast range of thymes, many of which are useful ornamentally, some in mixed borders and others in rockeries and paving.

5. In Segment 5 plant the second purple sage (D). This helps provide balance throughout the scheme.

Plant the apple mint (K) next. This tall growing mint has large oval furry leaves, a contrast in texture to the sage and bronze fennel. It produces underground spreading roots and is therefore best planted in a large bottomless flower pot or old bucket, sunk into the ground.

Plant the second golden sage (B). The four sages in this scheme provide balance, structure and winter colour.

6. In Segment 6 plant the remaining chives (E). Duplicating the grassy leaves of chives gives continuity throughout the scheme. Add 2 parsley (M), the feathery leaves of which are a good companion to other plants. Next plant the basil (L). Basil comes in a range of varieties, some with purple leaves and any of these would be suitable. In this case the round shiny leaves of the sweet basil contrast well with the apple mint and the parsley. Basil is not a hardy plant and should not be planted outside in colder areas until all risk of frost has passed.

7. The completed garden, if created in the spring, will take two or three months to mature.

ALTERNATIVE PLANTING SCHEME

This scheme includes a number of plants which are not reliably hardy. It will need a sheltered site in areas prone to winter frosts.

Segment 1
A. 6 thyme (*Thymus serpyllum* "Annie Hall") 3½in/9cm pots

Segment 2
B. 1 myrtle (*Myrtus communis* "Variegata"), 6½in/2 litre or 8½in/3 litre pot
C. 1 rosemary (*Rosmarinus officinalis*), 6½in/2 litre or 7½in/3 litre pot
D. 1 sage (*Salvia officinalis*), 6½in/2 litre or 7½in/3 litre pot

Segment 3
E. 3 garlic (*Allium sativum*) 3½in/9cm pots
F. 1 lovage (*Levisticum officinale*), 3½in/9cm pot
G. 2 lady's mantle (*Alchemilla mollis*), 3½in/9cm pots

Segment 4
H. 1 lavender (*Lanandula angustifolia* "Munstead"), 6½in/2 litre or 7½in/3 litre pot
I. 1 apple mint (*Mentha sauveolens*), 6½in/2 litre or 7½in/3 litre pot
J. 1 lavender (*Lavandula angustifolia* "Munstead"), 6½in/2 litre or 7½in/3 litre pot

Segment 5
D. 1 sage (*Salvia officinalis*) 6½in/2 litre or 7½in/3 litre pot
K. 1 variegated rue (*Ruta graveolens* "Variegata"), 5½in/1 litre or 6½in/2 litre pot
B. 1 sage (*Salvia officinalis*), 6½in/2 litre or 7½in/3 litre pot

Segment 6
E. 3 garlic (*Allium sativum*), 3½in/9cm pots
L. 1 tricoloured sage (*Salvia officinalis* "Tricolor"), 6½in/2 litre or 7½in/3 litre pot
M. 2 lady's mantle (*Alchemilla mollis*), 3½in/9cm pots

Herb Pots

Herbs are the perfect subjects for container gardening – their invasive tendency curtailed and requiring little watering, they seem at home. It is easy to bring the herbs near the kitchen door or into the house at the end of the growing season for use in the winter months. Subjects like French tarragon, which can look so untidy late in the season, can be hidden from view until the following year. Container groups are the ideal way of adding interest and maturity to a paved area. The common mistake is to dot them around a large area where they make little impact and often cause an obstruction. Draw them together into groups and place them strategically next to doorways or alongside a sitting area.

The Plants

1 bay (Laurus nobilis), 6½ in/2 litre or 7½ in/3 litre pot

1 French tarragon (Artemisia dracunculus), 5½ in/1 litre or 6½ in/2 litre pot

1 tricoloured sage (Salvia officinalis "Tricolor"), 6½ in/2 litre pot

3 gold-splashed marjoram (Origanum vulgare "Gold Tip"), 3½ in/9 cm pots

1 eau de Cologne mint (Mentha × piperita citrata), 5½ in/1 litre or 6½ in/2 litre pot

1 golden thyme (Thymus vulgaris aureus), 3½ in/9 cm pot

3 parsley (Petroselinum crispum), 3½ in/9 cm pots

1 chives (Allium schoenoprasum), 3½ in/9cm or 5½ in/1 litre pot

Materials

Three terracotta flower pots, one each of diameter 18 in/46 cm; 15½ in/39 cm; and 13 in/32 cm • 4 terracotta flowerpots, each 10½ in/27 cm in diameter • Crocks • Peat-based compost

Planting Plan

CARE

The parsley will need replacing annually, but the other plants will grow happily in their pots for up to three years with an annual top dressing of compost. Eventually, when a plant becomes too large, it could be planted into a larger container or planted out into the garden.

During very hot weather watering should be carried out at least twice a day, early in the morning and again in the evening. The pot should be watered until a puddle appears around the base of the pot. Feed with a liquid fertilizer every other week (each week for the parsley).

In colder climates, where prolonged frosts can be expected, the whole group should be moved to a sheltered part of the garden and given extra protection (the roots, being above ground, are more exposed to frost attack).

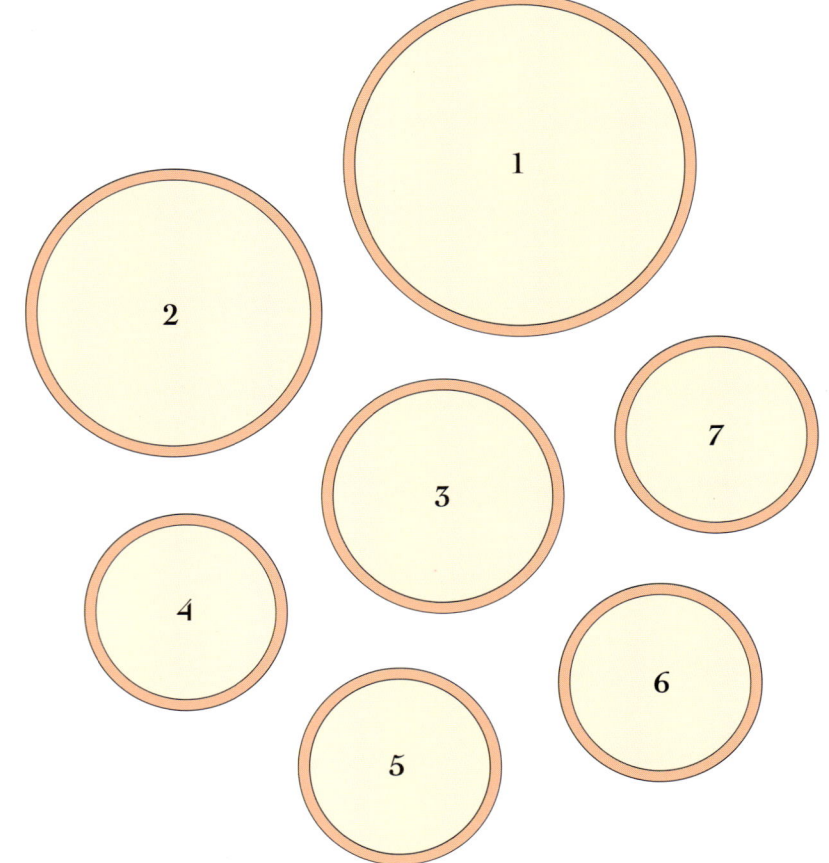

1. Start with the largest pot (Container 1). Cover the base of the container with a generous layer of crocks to aid drainage. Add the compost up to 1½ in/3 cm lower than the rim of the pot.

2. Remove the bay tree from its pot by inverting the plant and gently squeezing the rootball inside the plastic container. Tease the roots from the rootball to ensure the plant grows away well. Make sure the plant is planted to the same level as that in its original pot. Bay is not fully hardy and should be protected during cold weather.

3. Plant 3 gold splashed marjorams equally spaced around the edge of the container.

4. The marjorams will quickly cover the bare soil in the pot and even cascade down the sides.

5. The positioning of the group is critical to the overall effect. Here the gravel sets the terracotta off nicely.

6. Plant Container 2 with the French tarragon and place alongside the first. Plant eau de Cologne mint in Container 3 to make a striking contrast. This group is pleasing on its own and you may wish not to add further containers.

7. Plant 3 parsley plants in Container 4; a tricoloured sage in Container 5; golden thyme in Container 6; and chives in Container 7. Place these carefully around the outside of the group. The plants will need about two weeks in which to mature enough to harvest and two months to reach full maturity.

ALTERNATIVE PLANTING SCHEME

Container 1
1 rosemary (*Rosmarinus officinalis* "Miss Jessop's Upright"), 6½in/2 litre pot
3 prostrate thyme (*Thymus serpyllum* "Pink Chintz"), 3½in/9cm pots

Container 2
1 apple mint (*Mentha suaveolens*), 5½in/1 litre or 6½in/2 litre pot

Container 3
1 rue (*Ruta graveolens* "Jackman's Blue"), 6½in/2 litre pot

Container 4
1 basil (*Ocimum basilicum* "Green Ruffles"), 3½in/9cm or 5½in/1 litre pot

Container 5
1 lady's mantle (*Alchemilla mollis*), 3½in/9cm or 5½in/1 litre pot

Container 6
1 purple sage (*Salvia officinalis* "Purpurascens"), 6½in/2 litre or 7½in/3 litre pot

Container 7
2 French parsley (*Petroselinum crispum hortense*), 3½in/9cm pots

Start to plant • HERB GARDENS

Mint Diamonds

There are very many different varieties of mint now available but nearly all are aggressive colonizers and require some method to segregate them. The diamond pattern of bricks, not only looks good, but also helps to constrain the plants. The bold pattern of this feature may dominate the design of the garden in the near vicinity, so care must be taken in placing it. It would fit well into a patio, where the bricks could be used to pick up the colour of the bricks in the house, and, as a dominant feature, is particularly appropriate in a large paved area. It could also look good in a scree bed or gravel garden with stepping stones through the gravel for access.

Materials

144 bricks • Lean mix (6 parts builder's sand to 1 part cement) • Builder's line • Spirit level • Lump hammer • Spade • Builder's trowel • Garden trowel

CARE

An occasional trim when the herbs are in flower will help to keep the plants' shapes and stop any seed being set.

The Plants

2 spearmint (Mentha spicata), 5½ in/1 litre or 6½ in/2 litre pots

2 eau de Cologne mint (Mentha x piperita citrata), 5½ in/1 litre or 6½ in/2 litre pots

2 pineapple mint (Mentha suaveolens "Variegata"), 5½ in/1 litre or 6½ in/2 litre pots

1 apple mint (Mentha suaveolens), 5½ in/1 litre or 6½ in/2 litre pot

1. Dig out a trench 2ft/0.5m wide and 1ft/0.3m deep.

2. Lay the first layer of bricks, on a generous layer of lean mix, in the pattern shown. Use a builder's line to ensure a straight line.

3. Lay three layers of brick. The roots of mints are very invasive and the deeper you can go the better. Three layers should be enough, but to make sure go one or two layers deeper. It is essential that all the bricks are carefully pointed up, or an escape route will be provided for the plants.

4. Once the bricks have been laid, lay out the plants ready to be planted.

Planting Plan

ALTERNATIVE PLANTING SCHEME

This planting uses popular culinary herbs.

Diamond 1.
1 eau de Cologne mint (*Mentha × piperita citrata*), 5½in/1 litre or 6½in/2 litre pot

Diamond 2.
5 parsley (*Petroselinum crispum*), 3½in/9cm pots

Diamond 3.
5 thyme (*Thymus × citriodorus* "Silver Posie"), 3½in/9cm pots

Diamond 4.
1 rosemary (*Rosmarinus officinalis*), 5½in/1 litre or 6½in/2 litre pot

Diamond 5.
4 basil (*Ocimum basilicum*), 3½in/9cm pots

Diamond 6.
5 chives (*Allium schoenoprasum*), 3½in/9cm pots

Diamond 7
1 purple sage (*Salvia officinalis* "Purpurascens"), 5½in/1 litre or 6½in/2 litre pot

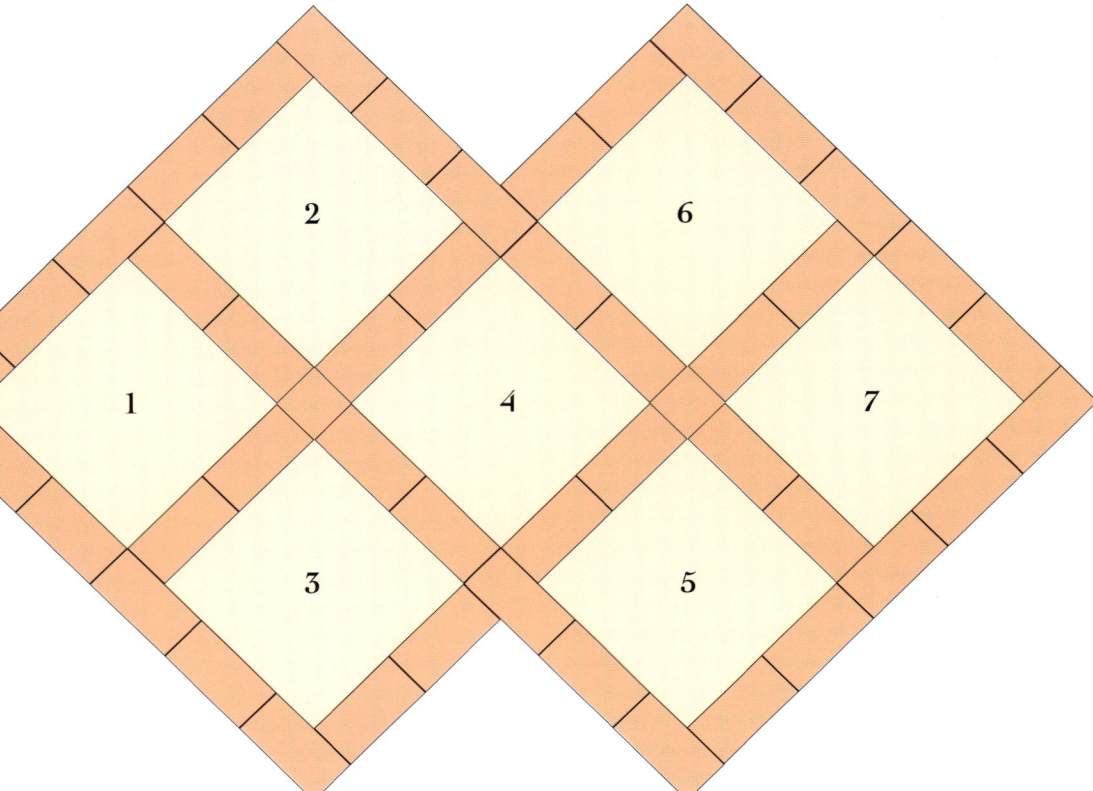

1. Break each plant out of its pot by inverting it and squeezing the plastic pot. Before planting, tease the roots out from the rootball to ensure the plant grows away well. In Diamond 1 plant one spearmint.

2. Plant one of the variegated pineapple mints in Diamond 2; and one of the fragrant eau de Cologne mints in Diamond 3.

3. In Diamond 4 plant the apple mint and in Diamond 5 the second pineapple mint.

4. In Diamond 6 plant the second eau de Cologne mint. Finally plant the other spearmint plant in Diamond 7.

5. Once planted, it will take two or three months for the scheme to take shape.

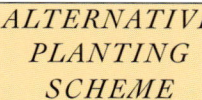

ALTERNATIVE PLANTING SCHEME

Diamond 1.
1 basil mint (*Mentha × piperita citrata* "Basil"), 5½in/1 litre or 6½in/2 litre pot

Diamond 2.
1 Moroccan mint (*Mentha spicata* "Moroccan"), 5½in/1 litre or 6½in/2 litre pot

Diamond 3.
1 pennyroyal (*Mentha pulegium*), 5½in/1 litre pot

Diamond 4.
1 ginger mint (*Mentha × gracilis*), 5½in/1 litre or 6½in/2 litre pot

Diamond 5.
1 curly mint (*Mentha spicata crispa*), 5½in/1 litre pot

Diamond 6.
1 pennyroyal (*Mentha pulegium*), 5½in/1 litre pot

Diamond 7
1 black peppermint (*Mentha × piperita*), 5½in/1 litre or 6½in/2 litre pot

Herb Wheel

This traditional design is a simple but very effective way of growing herbs, and is often used as the central feature in an ornamental vegetable garden or potager. An attractive idea is to place a small sundial, bird table or small statue in the centre.

The Plants

A. *3 golden marjoram (Origanum vulgare "Aureum"), 3½ in/9 cm pots*

B. *2 thyme (Thymus × citriodorus "Silver Posie"), 3½ in/9 cm pots*

C. *2 chives (Allium schoenoprasum), 3½ in/9 cm pots*

D. *4 parsley (Petroselinum crispum), 3½ in/9 cm pots*

E. *1 basil (Ocimum basilicum), 3½ in/9 cm or 5½ in/1 litre pot*

F. *1 pineapple mint (Mentha suaveolens "Variegata"), 5½ in/1 litre 6½ in/2 litre pot*

G. *3 golden thyme (Thymus vulgaris aureus), 3½ in/9 cm pots*

H. *1 Corsican rosemary (Rosmarinus officinalis "Corsican Blue"), 6½ in/2 litre or 7½ in/3 litre pot*

I. *1 coriander (Coriandum sativum), 3½ in/9 cm or 5½ in/1 litre cm pot*

J. *1 black peppermint (Mentha × piperita), 6½ in/2 litre or 8½ in/3 litre pot*

Materials

71 bricks • Lean mix (6 parts builder's sand to 1 part cement) • Builder's line • Spirit level • Lump hammer • Spade • Builder's trowel • Garden trowel • Stake

1. Drive a stake into the ground and loosely attach a 30 in/76 cm length of builder's line. Using the metal marker at the other end of the line, carefully mark out the inner circle of the wheel "rim".

2. Dig out a shallow trench and line with a lean mix.

3. Lay bricks, using the builder's line to ensure the circle is followed. Check that each brick is level using a spirit level.

4. Once the "rim" has been laid, mark out the "spokes" and line these with the lean mix. Lay the bricks as shown.

5. Lay the plants out on the completed wheel in their positions ready for planting, by following the Planting Plan.

Planting Plan

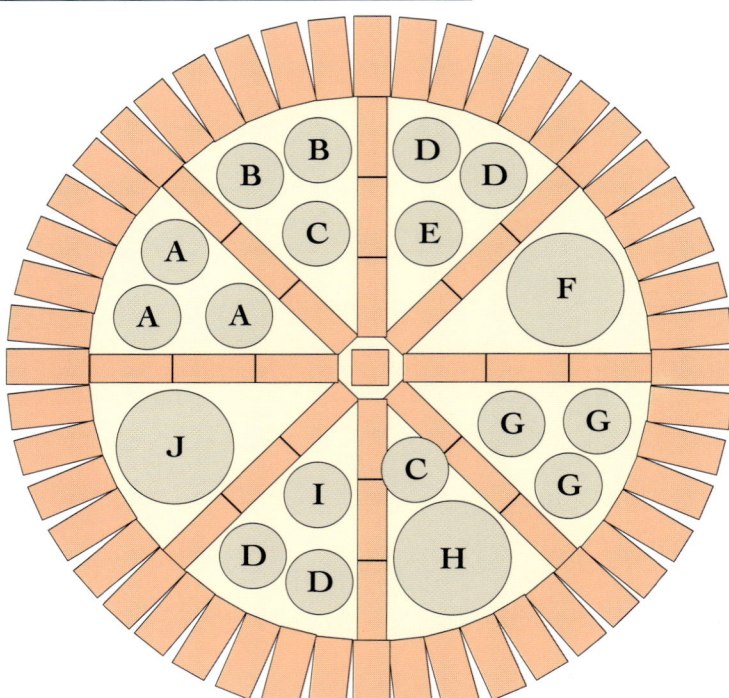

ALTERNATIVE PLANTING SCHEME

1st Segment
A. 3 wild strawberry (*Fragaria vesca*), 3½in/9cm pots

2nd Segment
B. 2 prostrate thyme (*Thymus serpyllum* "Annie Hall"), 3½in/9cm pots
C. 1 garlic chives (*Allium tuberosum*), 3½in/9cm pot

3rd Segment
D. 2 parsley (*Petroselinum crispum*), 3½in/9cm pots
E. 1 cinnamon basil (*Ocimum basilicum* "Cinnamon"), 3½in/9cm or 5½in/1 litre pot

4th Segment
F. 1 prostrate rosemary (*Rosmarinus lavandulaceus*), 6½in/2 litre or 7½in/3 litre pot

5th Segment
G. 3 alpine strawberry (*Fragaria vesca* "Semperflorens"), 3½in/9cm pots

6th Segment
C. 1 tree onion (*Allium cepa proliferum*), 3½in/9cm pot
H. 1 lavender (*Lavandula angustifolia* "Hidcote"), 5½in/1 litre or 6½in/2 litre pot

7th Segment
I. 1 chervil (*Anthriscus cerefolium*), 3½in/9cm pot
D. 2 parsley (*Petroselinum crispum*), 3½in/9cm pots

8th Segment
J. 1 purple sage (*Salvia officinalis* "Purpurascens"), 6½in/2 litre or 7½in/3 litre pot

1. To remove each plant from its pot invert it gently and squeeze the pot. Tease out the roots before planting as this encourages the plant to grow away quickly.

Start by planting the 3 golden marjoram (A) in one of the "wedges". The golden leaves will contrast well with the black peppermint which will be planted in the neighbouring segment.

2. In the next segment plant 2 thymes (B) and 1 chives (C). The small variegated leaves of the thymes add freshness to the scheme. The grass-like leaves of the chives are essential in any scheme, adding that contrasting shape. The flowers, which bloom all summer if deadheaded regularly, associate well with many colour schemes.

3. Plant 2 parsley (D) and 1 basil (E) in the next segment. The parsley associates well with the neighbouring plants, and the basil adds freshness to the scheme, its round leaves contrasting well with the grass-like leaves of the chives.

4. The pineapple mint (F) is planted in the next segment. This variegated plant adds texture and shape and complements the variegation in the thyme.

5. Next plant the 3 golden thymes (G) in the neighbouring segments. These are chosen to balance the golden marjoram in the opposite segment of the wheel.

6. In the segment next to the golden thymes plant the other chives plant (C), to add continuity through the plan, and the Corsican rosemary (H). This low growing rosemary will grow out over the "rim" of the wheel as well as offer a contrast to the golden thyme and chives.

7. The 2 remaining parsley (D) and the coriander (I) are planted in the next "wedge". The deeply divided coriander leaves will balance the parsley growing in the opposite segment and complement the parsley growing alongside.

8. Plant the black peppermint (J), or the similar Eau de Cologne mint, to add a welcome colour contrast. Like all mints, this plant is invasive so plant it inside a bottomless flowerpot or bucket with a depth of not less than 12 in/30 cm.

9. The final scheme will take two to three months to develop, if planted in the spring.

CARE

Parsley, basil and coriander are all annuals and will need replacing each year. The basil and coriander are both tender and should not be planted in cold areas until after the danger of frosts has passed. The parsley and basil will benefit from the occasional liquid feed.

Start to plant • HERB GARDENS

Herbs in Paving

Paving offers ideal conditions for growing the many herbs that prefer hot dry conditions, and leaves brushed against or crushed by passing feet release their heady aromas into the air. The checkerboard pattern, used in this project, could be replicated throughout a patio by using light and darker coloured slabs. The stepping stone route through this herb bed could be reorganized into a more straightforward route through the herbs, or other interesting designs for a path could be developed.

Materials

Six 18 in/46 cm square paving slabs
- Hardcore • Concrete cement mix
- Spirit level • Builder's trowel
- Garden trowel • Lump hammer

CARE

Trimming over the thyme in the spring is all that should be required, unless the sage becomes leggy, then this should be cut hard back.

The Plants

A. *1 Moroccan mint (Mentha spicata "Moroccan"), 5½ in/14 cm or 6½ in/2 litre pot*

B. *3 oregano (Origanum vulgare), 5½ in/1 litre pots*

C. *1 tricoloured sage (Salvia officinalis "Tricolor"), 6½ in/2 litre or 8½ in/3 litre pot*

D. *2 thyme (Thymus "Doone Valley"), 5½ in/1 litre pots*

E. *4 camomile (Chamaemelum nobile "Treneague"), 3½ in/9 cm pots*

F. *4 Corsican mint (Mentha requienii), 3½ in/9 cm pots*

1. Excavate a hole the size and shape of the paving slab to be laid. Line this with hardcore and add five spots of cement. Lay the paving slab onto this and, using the spirit and the lump hammer ensure the whole thing is level. Follow this procedure for all the paving slabs in the scheme.

2. Lay the plants in position, ready for planting, following the Planting Plan.

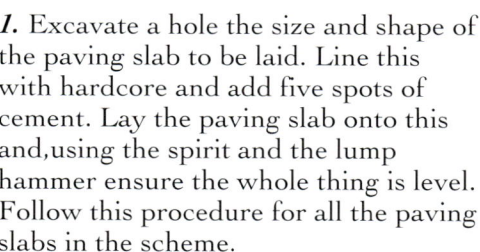

Planting Plan

ALTERNATIVE PLANTING SCHEME

A. 4 dwarf marjoram (*Origanum vulgare* "Nanum"), 3½in/9cm or 5½in/1 litre pots
B. 3 lady's mantle (*Alchemilla mollis*), 3½in/9cm or 5½in/1 litre pots
C. 3 nasturtium (*Tropaeolum majus*), 3½in/9cm pots
D. 1 eau de Cologne mint (*Mentha × piperita citrata*), 5½in/1 litre or 6½in/2 litre pot
E. 1 sage (*Salvia officinalis*), 6½in/2 litre or 7½in/3 litre pot
F. 4 pot marigold (*Calendula officinalis*), 3½in/9cm or 5½in/1 litre pots

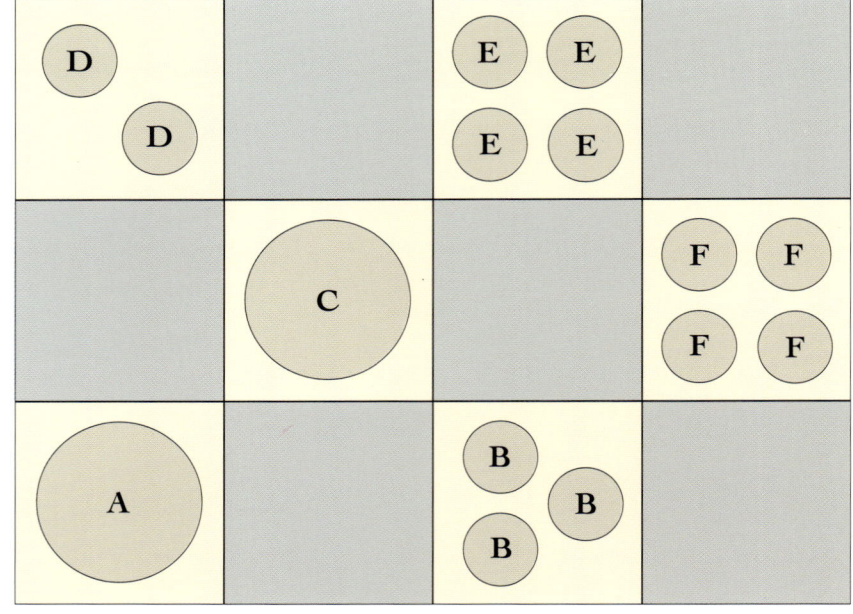

1. Remove each plant from its pot by first inverting the plant and then carefully squeezing the outside. Tease the roots out to ensure the plant grows away well, before planting.
  Plant the Moroccan mint (A) in the bottom left hand square, and the 3 oregano (B) in the square next to it. Plant the tricoloured sage (C) in the centre square.

2. Plant the 2 thymes (D) in the top left hand square, the 4 camomile (E) in the square next to the thymes, and in the remaining square, the 4 Corsican mints (F).

3. The finished project will take 2 or 3 months to develop, if planted in the spring.

Hanging Basket

Hanging baskets full of lobelia, ivy-leaved geraniums, impatiens and trailing fuchsias have become a popular summer feature. A hanging basket of herbs is not only attractive, but very useful, and can be brought into the kitchen and hung from a hook whenever culinary herbs are needed. Many of the herbs are evergreen so this basket can be used all year round.

Materials

A hanging basket, 23½ in/60 cm in diameter • Moss • A square of plastic sheet, perforated for drainage • Peat-based compost

CARE

Hanging baskets dry out very quickly, so they cannot be over-watered. In warm weather they will require watering at least three times a day. A good method of watering is to use a large plastic soft drinks bottle and a chair to stand on (and then to sit on when the job is done!). Wind can have a severe desiccating effect and in severe conditions the hanging basket should be removed to a sheltered spot.

The plants used here can only stay in the hanging basket for a season (one year if planted in the spring and brought in the house for winter). Some of the plants can be planted out into the garden once the basket is finished.

The Plants

A. *2 purple sage (Salvia officinalis "Purpurascens"), 3½ in/9 cm pots*

B. *2 parsley (Petroselinum crispum), 3½ in/9 cm pots*

C. *2 marjoram (Marjorum vulgare "Gold Tip"), 3½ in/9 cm pots*

D. *1 rosemary (Rosmarinus officinalis), 3½ in/1 litre pot*

E. *1 chives (Allium schoenoprasum), 3½ in/9 cm or 3½ in/1 litre pot*

F. *2 thyme (Thymus × citriodorus "Silver Posie"), 3½ in/9 cm pots*

G. *1 basil (Ocimum basilicum), 3½ in/9 cm pot*

1. Stand the hanging basket in a medium-sized flowerpot, to hold it steady and upright.

2. Line the base with moss, bringing it about a third of the way up the basket side. Ensure the moss is well consolidated.

3. Cut a plastic sheet from the compost bag. Place the plastic sheeting in the base of the basket. This will help to keep moisture in and prevent the basket from drying out too quickly.

Planting Plan

1. Position the first layer of plants in their growing position. Tease the roots out to encourage good root development Plant 2 purple sage (A), 2 parsley (B) and 2 marjoram (C) in positions shown in the Planting Plan.

2. Build the moss up round the sides to the top of the basket.

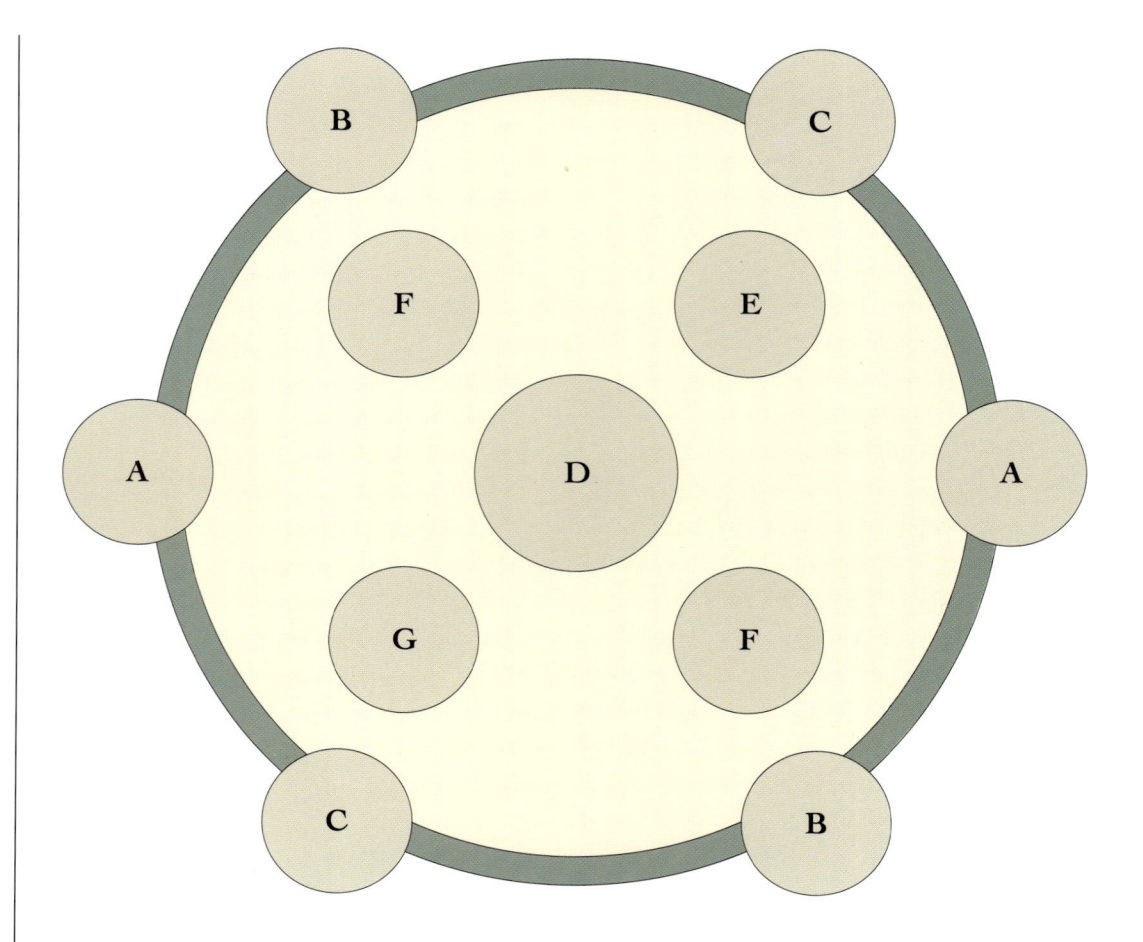

3. Add compost into the centre of the "nest" created by the moss.

4. Plant 1 rosemary (D), 1 chives (E), 2 thymes (F), and 1 basil (G) in the positions shown in the Planting Plan.

ALTERNATIVE PLANTING SCHEME

This unusual planting scheme requires longer wires to support the basket in order to allow room for the fennel to grow. It can be controlled by simply cutting the top off periodically.

A. 2 golden feverfew (*Tanacetum parthenium* "Aureum"), 3½in/9cm pots

B. 2 coriander (*Coriandrum sativum*), 3½in/9cm pots

C. 2 wild strawberry (*Fragaria vesca*), 3½in/9cm pots

D. 1 French tarragon (*Artemisia dracunculus*), 3½in/9cm pot

E. 1 chives (*Allium schoenoprasum*), 3½in/9cm or 5½in/1 litre pot

F. 2 bronze fennel (*Foeniculum vulgare* "Purpureum"), 3½in/9cm or 5½in/1 litre pots

G. 1 curry plant (*Helichrysum italicum*), 3½in/9cm or 5½in/1 litre pot

5. The finished basket will take a few weeks to develop to a position when the herbs can be harvested for the kitchen.

Herb Border

*T*his herb border should be south- or south-west facing and backed by a fence or wall, and if the herbs are to be fully utilised, they should be grown within easy reach of where they will be needed, usually the kitchen.

The herb garden's inherent untidiness could spoil the view of the garden, but by carefully selecting the plants and positioning them with care in the border the herbs will blend together or with other garden plants to create an attractive planted border.

The Plants

A. *3 variegated wild strawberry (Fragaria vesca "Variegata"), 3½ in/9 cm pots*

B. *1 chives (Allium schoenoprasum), 3½ in/9 cm or 5½ in/1 litre pot*

C. *5 sweet cicely (Myrrhis odorata), 3½ in/9 cm pots*

D. *7 catmint (Nepeta racemosa, syn. Nepeta mussinii), 3½ in/9 cm pots*

E. *1 angelica (Angelica archangelica), 3½ in/9 cm or 5½ in/1 litre pot*

CARE

This scheme will need little maintenance and should give pleasure for a number of years before any changes are needed.

If the sage looks a little "leggy" in the spring, cut it hard back. The artemisia must be cut to within 2 in/5 cm of the ground every spring as soon as growth appears close to the base, if not then it will grow "birds nests" on the end of each branch and become large and untidy. Trim the catmint over with a pair of shears when the flowers have finished and it will flower again (the plant can be encouraged to flower all summer).

F. *2 bergamot (Monarda didyma "Cambridge Scarlet"), 3½ in/9 cm pots*

G. *1 iris (Iris foetidissima "Variegata"), 5½ in/1 litre or 6½ in/2 litre pot*

H. *1 pineapple mint (Mentha sauveolens "Variegata"), 5½ in/1 litre or 6½ in/2 litre pot*

S1. *2 rosemary (Rosmarinus officinalis), 6½ in/2 litre or 7½ in/3 litre pots*

Materials

Garden spade • Rake • Garden trowel
• Wheelbarrow • Vine eyes
• Galvanized wire

S2. *2 purple sage (Salvia officinalis "Purpurascens"), 6½ in/2 litre or 8½ in/3 litre pots*

S3. *2 rue (Ruta graveolens "Jackman's Blue"), 5½ in/1 litre or 6½ in/2 litre pots*

S4. *1 golden sage (Salvia officinalis "Icterina") 6½ in/2 litre or 8½ in/3 litre pot*

S5. *1 artemisia (Artemisia "Powis Castle"), 5½ in/1 litre or 6½ in/2 litre pot*

1. Dig over the area to be planted (about 16 ft/5 m x 8 ft/2.5 m), to one spade's depth, incorporating sharp sand (¼ in/25 mm spread across the surface before digging in). Rake over the surface to form a fine tilth.

Start to plant • HERB GARDENS

Planting Plan

ALTERNATIVE PLANTING SCHEME

This scheme will require a more sheltered site and the caraway will need a fresh planting annually.

A. 1 eau de Cologne mint (*Mentha × piperata citrata*), 5½in/1 litre or 6½in/2 litre pot
B. 1 French tarragon (*Artemisia dracunculus*), 5½in/1 litre or 6½in/2 litre pot
C. 5 caraway (*Carum carvi*), 3½in/9cm pots
D. 7 chervil (*Anthriscus cerefolium*), 3½in/9cm pots
E. 1 fennel (*Foeniculum vulgare*), 3½in/9cm pot
F. 2 bergamot (*Monarda fistulosa*), 3½in/9cm pots
G. 1 chives (*Allium schoenaprasum*), 3½in/9cm or 5½in/1 litre pot
H. 1 eau de Cologne mint (*Mentha × piperata citrata*), 5½in/1 litre or 6½in/2 litre pot
S1. 2 bay (*Laurus nobilis*), 6½in/2 litre or 7½in/3 litre pots
S2. 2 golden sage (*Salvia officinalis* "Icterina"), 6½in/2 litre or 7½in/3 litre pots
S3. 2 lavender (*Lavandula angustifolia* "Munstead"), 5½in/1 litre or 6½in/2 litre pots
S4. 1 purple sage (*Salvia officinalis* "Purpurascens"), 6½in/2 litre or 7½in/3 litre pot
S5. 1 artemisia (*Artemisia* "Powis Castle"), 5½in/1 litre or 6½in/2 litre pot

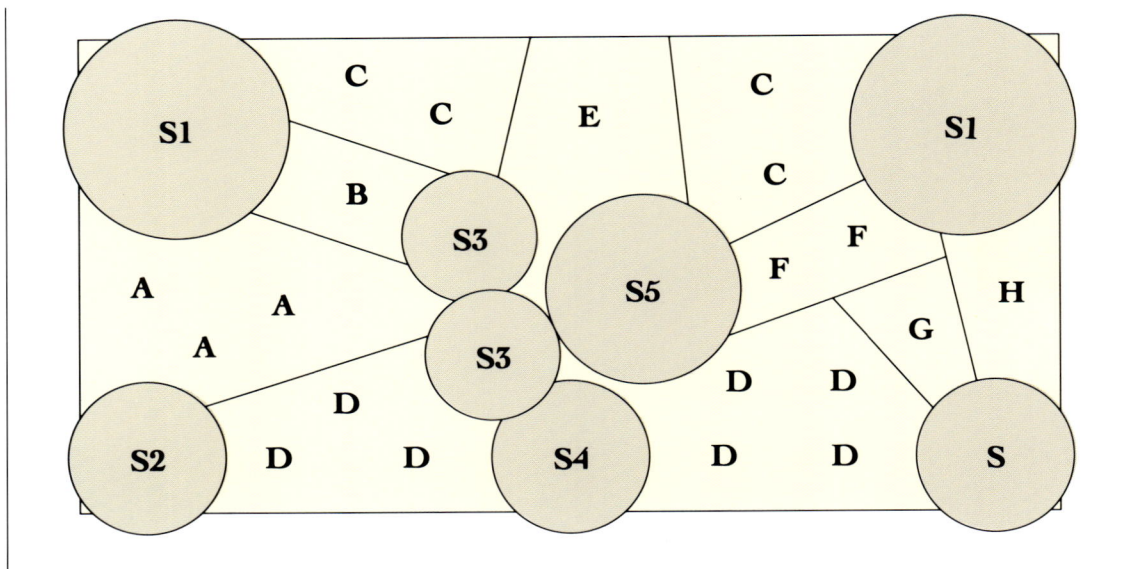

1. First, plant the structural plants. Some are evergreen and provide all year round colour to the scheme. Pick out the key points first, in this case the corners, with the structural plants. Plant the 2 rosemary (S1) and the 2 purple sage (S2) in the corners as shown on the Planting Plan. Then fill out the central area with the 2 rue (S3), a golden sage (S4) and the artemisia (S5).

2. When planting, ensure the roots are teased out to ensure they grow away well.

3. Plant up the first layer of in-fill plants. The 7 catmint (D) will flower for most of the summer, if trimmed over occasionally with a pair of shears. It compliments the sage at each corner and contrasts well with the golden sage planted in the centre. The rue has a fine blue finish to its leaves which picks up the blue of the catmint and carries it through the scheme. The variegation in the pineapple mint (H) adds a bright contrast. Plant it in a bottomless flowerpot or bucket.

4. The second layer of in-fill planting completes the plan and includes some of the larger plants. Angelica (E) will grow to 5 ft/1.5 m or more and has been given plenty of room at the back of the border. The feathery leaves of the 5 sweet cicely (C) infill nicely between the tall angelica and the medium level. The 3 variegated wild strawberry (A) balance the variegated apple mint on the opposite side of the border. The sword leaves of the iris (G) add impact on the right and are picked up by the grass-like leaves of the chives (B) on the left. The plan is finished with a bold splash of red provided by the flowers of the 2 bergamot (F).

5. Once the border has been planted up, mulching between plants will keep weeds down, maintain moisture and provide a background for the plants. In this instance, forest bark has been used, but pea shingle would work equally well and may be more appropriate, dependent upon the overall design. The ground must be thoroughly wetted before mulch is applied. As it acts as an insulation, it can just as easily keep the ground bone dry as it can keep it moist. Also, it must be a fair depth (2 in/5 cm ideally) to ensure any weed seeds are kept in the dark and therefore do not germinate.

6. The final scheme will mature quite quickly if planted in the spring or early summer.

Herbs in a Mixed Border

Herbs are fine plants for a mixed border, so why allocate them a separate garden? This project explores how herbs can be used in a border with other flowering plants. It is an excellent way of growing herbs within an overall garden scene. Any herbs not grown in the border can be grown in pots on the patio. The border is 25ft/7.6m long by about 9ft/2.6m deep and should ideally be south- or west-facing. If your border is east-facing then it could also be used, so long as it is backed by a 6ft/1.8m high fence and not a tall house wall or high hedge.

The Plants

S1. 2 cotton lavender (*Santolina chamaecyparissus*), 6½ in/1 litre pots

S2. 2 Mexican orange blossom (*Choisya ternata*), 7½ in/3 litre pots or bigger

S3. 2 sage (*Salvia officinalis*), 6½ in/2 litre or 7½ in/3 litre pots

S4. 1 Californian lilac (*Ceanothus thyrsiflorus*), 7½ in/3 litre pot or bigger

S5. 6 lavender (*Lavandula angustifolia*), 5½ in/1 litre or 6½ in/2 litre pots

S6. 1 rosemary (*Rosmarinus officinalis*), 6½ in/2 litre or 7½ in/3 litre pot

A. 3 bergamot (*Monarda didyma*), 3½ in/9 cm pots

B. 3 chives (*Allium schoenoprasum*), 3½ in/9 cm or 5½ in/1 litre pots

C. 2 cranesbill (*Geranium* × *riversleaianum* "Russell Prichard"), 5½ in/1 litre or 6½ in/2 litre pots

D. 2 fennel (*Foeniculum vulgare*), 3½ in/9 cm or 5½ in/1 litre pots

E. 1 spearmint (*Mentha spicata*), 5½ in/1 litre or 6½ in/2 litre pot

Materials

Garden spade • Rake • Garden trowel
• Galvanized wire • Vine eyes

F. *2 heuchera (Heuchera "Palace Purple"), 3½ in/9 cm or 5½ in/1 litre pots*

G. *2 parsley (Petroselinum crispum), 3½ in/9 cm pots*

H. *2 iris (Iris pallida "Variegata"), 3½ in/9 cm or 5½ in/1 litre pots*

I. *2 euphorbia (Euphorbia characias wulfenii), 3½ in/9 cm or 5½ in/1 litre pots*

J. *3 lady's mantle (Alchemilla mollis), 3½ in/9 cm pots*

K. *1 pineapple mint (Mentha suaveolens "Variegata"), 5½ in/1 litre or 6½ in/2 litre pot*

L. *1 French tarragon (Artemisia dracunculus), 3½ in/9 cm or 5½ in/1 litre pot*

K1. *1 juniper (Juniperus communis "Hibernica"), 7½ in/3 litre pot or bigger*

C1. *2 vine (Vitis vinifera "Black Hamburg"), 6½ in/2 litre or 7½ in/3 litre pots*

1. Dig over the area to be planted to one spade's depth.

Start to plant • HERB GARDENS

43

2. Incorporate a mixture of peat, well-rotted farmyard manure (or compost) and sharp sand in equal parts (put a layer ¼ in/25 mm deep, spread across the surface before digging in). Rake over the surface of the soil to form a fine tilth.

3. Vines always require support, and this can best be achieved by using vine screw eyes and galvanized wire. Either screw the the vine eyes into the fence pots or attach to a wall by drilling holes and inserting rawlplugs. Galvanized wire should then be stretched horizontally between the eyes. The wire should be 18 in/46 cm apart vertically. This is the best form of support as it blends with the vine, allowing you to enjoy the plant and what is keeping it in place.

1. Plant the main structural plants – the bones of the scheme. These are the evergreens which will provide all year round interest and include 2 Mexican orange blossom (S2), a Californian lilac, (S4), 2 sage (S3), and 2 cotton lavender (S1).

2. Plant the in-fill structural plants. Once the key structural plants have been planted the smaller evergreens are used to ensure a good spread throughout the scheme. The 2 grapevines (C1) on the back fence or wall, although not evergreen, will grow thick woolly stems in time and these will add winter interest, along with the Irish Juniper (K1), the rosemary (S6) and 6 lavenders (S5). The upright shape of the Irish juniper is an important contrast for the round shape of the ceanothus and adds height to the overall scheme.

Planting Plan

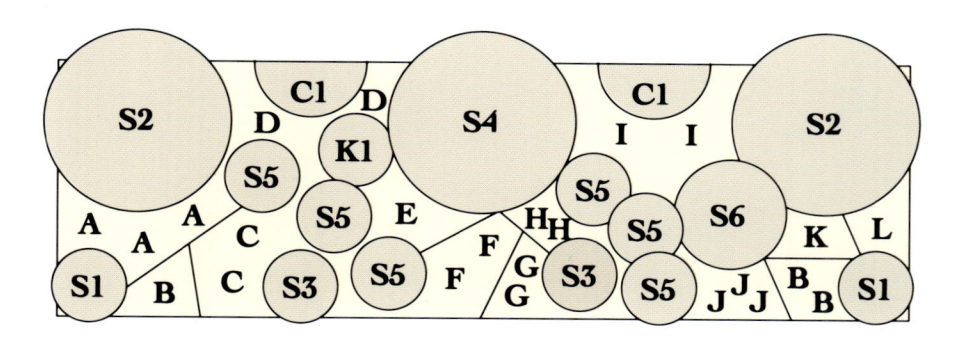

3. Smaller herbaceous perennials and shrubs, grown for their flowers and colour, are planted around the structural plants to add flair. This first group will bring in rich reds with the bergamot (A) and deep purple with the heucheras (F).

The French tarragon (L) should be planted in a large bottomless flowerpot or bucket to prevent its invasive runners spreading too far. Plant the 2 fennel (D), the 2 euphorbia (I), and the 2 lady's mantle (J).

CARE

Trim the cotton lavender and lavender after flowering, with shears or secateurs, to maintain shape. Tie new growth from the vines into wires in late summer or autumn. Remove dead foliage each spring. Replace the parsley annually.

4. The final group of in-fill plants includes 3 chives (B), whose flowers can be used to brighten up a salad, and the feathery foliage of the 2 parsley (G) which, as an annual, will need replacing each year. The spearmint (E) and the pineapple mint (K) should be planted in a large bottomless flowerpot or bucket to contain their invasive roots. Plant the variegated iris (H) and the cranesbills (C) in the border. The cranesbills will flower their heart out all summer long and they combine well with the form and flower colour of chives, an excellent front of the border perennial.

5. Once planted the scheme will take three or four months to establish itself (if planted in the spring) and about four years to mature.

Window Box

Herbs need to be close at hand for the creative cook and having them just outside the kitchen window is the perfect solution. They can easily be looked after in this situation and, as long as they are well watered, and replaced when too big, a large number can be grown in a small space. Try a window box at each window, perhaps adding a similar pelargonium into each window box, to provide continuity.

The Plants

1 pineapple mint (Mentha suaveolens "Variegata"), 5½ in/1 litre or 6½ in/2 litre pot

1 rosemary (Rosmarinus officinalis), 6½ in/2 litre pot

1 thyme (Thymus × citriodorus "Silver Posie"), 3½ in/9 cm pot

1 purple sage (Salvia officinalis "Purpurascens"), 6½ in/2 litre pot

1 marjoram (Origanum vulgare "Gold Tip"), 3½ in/9 cm pot

2 parsley (Petroselinum crispum), 3½ in/9 cm pots

1 chives (Allium schoenoprasum), 3½ in/9 cm pot

Materials

A window box, 30 in/76 cm × 7 in/18 cm high × 8 in/21 cm wide • Crocks

• Peat-based compost

• Garden trowel

CARE

As the plants are crammed in for effect, they can remain in the container for one year (if planted in spring and brought indoors in winter). The perennials and shrubs could be planted out into the garden.